Tom –

Thank you for all the ef[...] on the Carlsbad Boy[...] & Girls Club Campaign with your Rancho Carlsbad Team!

God Bless

[illegible] "2008"

# Half Time

Greg Nelson

GRN Publishing
Carlsbad, CA

Published by GRN Publishing
Carlsbad, CA

Publisher's Cataloging-in-Publication Data
Nelson, Greg.

Half time. – Carlsbad, CA : GRN Pub., 2006.

p. ; cm.
ISBN: 0-9725402-0-2
ISBN13: 978-0-9725402-0-9

1. American poetry. I. Title.

PS3614 .N45 2006
811/.608-dc22 2006922356

Printed in China
10 09 08 07 06 • 5 4 3 2 1

To my wife Barbi
*Thank you for your love and support.*

To Chad, Brooke, Gregory Jr. and Jenna Lee
*I am proud to be your father.*

# Contents

## About the Author

Greg Nelson is the co-founder of two highly successful orthopedic companies. First was DonJoy Orthopedics, which he sold in 1987 to Smith & Nephew, Inc. and is currently listed on the New York Stock Exchange as D.J. Orthopedics.

As President, he helped to lead the "DonJoy Team" to revenue of over $70 million. Then, as co-founder and past Chairman of the Board, he helped build Breg, Inc. to over $60 million in revenue. Breg, Inc. was acquired in 2003 by Orthofix, Inc.

Nelson was named the Carlsbad Citizen of the Year in 1991, received the National Medallion from Boys & Girls Clubs of America in 2001, and was named the Carlsbad Chamber of Commerce Philanthropist of the Year in 2006. Currently, he and his wife, Barbi, are co-chairing a $6 million campaign to build an additional Boys & Girls Club in South Carlsbad. He is an active member of the Rancho del Rey Community Church, and owns Gregorio's Restaurant in Carlsbad, California.

# Foreword

God has blessed me! First, with the mother he chose for me: Mercedes Olsen Nelson Piety. A strong-willed woman, who after my father left when I was nine, raised my brother Doug and me through her hard work, persistence and pride. Her love and unfailing loyalty will always be the cornerstones of my personality.

I have been writing since Mr. Taber assigned my sixth grade class at Pine Avenue School in Carlsbad, California, to write a Limerick. That assignment was my first poem, and my first effort at writing.

> "There once was a lady from Asia,
> She didn't have money to pay ya,
> She couldn't pay her taxes
> So she ended with the axes,
> The little old lady from Asia."

Because my mom was always working, she arranged to have my brother Doug and I walk to the Carlsbad Boys Club every day after school. The Boys Club would become our safe shelter, afternoon and evening play area, and overall life environment for most of our youth. It was through sports and the club activities that Doug and I kept busy, and the Boys Club staff became our early mentors. Men like Conti Rodriguez, Carlos Ramirez, John Penrod and John "Duck Brains" DeWitt were all helpful in steering us away from trouble.

When Doug Hall became Executive Director for the Boys Club, I found my first leadership and professional mentor.

Mr. Hall gave me my first job, taught me much about responsibility and management, and is still a mentor and friend to this day. He was also the first person to explain to me that you can't get to Heaven by earning good deeds points in life. "Brownie points won't get you to Heaven, Greg." Mr. Hall said. "Salvation is a Gift not earned!"

The Boys Club certainly was the framework for my young life, and I will always be thankful for this wonderful organization. I wrote my second poem, that I can remember, as a Boys Club member, entitled "The Boys Club Is..."

"The Boys Club is a place to come,
    a place to grow,
A place to have fun
    With the people you know.

Where guidance through friendship
    Is our motto,
And this is the key
    For the success of tomorrow."

Working as a Boys Club employee was my first career. As a Gym Instructor and Aquatics Director at the Carlsbad Boys Club and Branch Manager, Assistant Executive Director at the San Dieguito Boys and Girls Clubs and then Executive Director of the Carlsbad Boys Club, I learned organizational and motivational skills along with life's #1 business lesson – The Importance of People! As I watched San Dieguito Boys Club volunteer board members, Doug Allred, Terry Lingenfelder, Ray Griset, Charlie Clark, Don Frick and Steve Fletcher, lead the most dynamic youth organization in the area, I learned the importance of teamwork, a positive attitude and raising the high bar in your expectations. Doug Allred in particular, became a role model for me, not only as a businessman, but also as a community and family leader.

Early job experiences at the Boys Club and other jobs taught me the importance of faith, charity and giving, while the experience as a Bellman at the La Costa Country Club, taught me the importance of service and going the extra mile.

God has certainly blessed me! While playing recreational basketball, I was able to meet hundreds of terrific guys; people I still see today throughout San Diego County. And it was through basketball that I met my first two business partners at DonJoy, Ken Reed and Mark Nordquist. Although Mark was only involved for a short while, the ten years that Ken and I worked together, were both the best and most difficult of my life. Working through adversity and financial pressure taught me much about partnerships, friendships, trust, love and perseverance. Ken also taught me so much about generosity, family and loyalty. Thank you, Ken.

Good partners and Teamwork are important in everything we do, and I have been blessed with the greatest of partners. Brad Mason has been a friend since we met at the Boys Club in 1970 and a business partner both at DonJoy and at BREG, Inc. We have watched each other grow, experienced highs and lows together, and my family considers Brad a "family member." You will not find a more honest, talented, smart, straight-up person in the world. I have always felt that Brad could be a fortune 500 CEO if he wanted to be. Bill Bue, a one is a million personality, is the best at making others want to buy something from him. He doesn't move left...he doesn't move right.... BREG would not have succeeded with out Bill Bue. Bill Hopson (the Chief) has kept us solid. Always with both feet on the ground, (even when rebounding), Bill provides sound thinking; he seldom "takes the fake." Jeff Mason, certainly the smartest, self-taught engineer in the world, is the consummate team player. I've watched Jeff design a million dollar product in seconds. To all my partners, a sincere thank you. Also, thank you to Pat, Steve, Todd, Dean, Ray, Mark and so many other team members. I appreciate you all. Thanks for the support!

The real benefit of my business life is the people that I meet. From the early days of "working" the convention and trade show hotel bars, to golf tournaments, educational symposiums and wine dinners at restaurants and in my home, I have been blessed to meet and foster many lifetime friendships. From Gary Losse, Rob Heidt and their families to innumerable other special doctors, thank you; I started to write more names but stopped, afraid to leave someone out. You guys know who you are. I love you, and thank you for your friendship.

God has blessed me with a wonderful family. Thank you, Barbi. You are an angel on earth, not only to me, but to so many other people. Your love and support is the rock upon which I stand. You are the most wonderful wife in the world! I love you. I love my four children. To my sons, Chad and Gregory, Jr., thank you for your effort in all that you do. I could not be more proud of you both! Our years together with basketball and other sports are some of the fondest memories I have. Jenna Lee! What a beautiful lady you have become, both inside and out. I look forward to watching you grow; and you know I love you and am always proud of you. Thank you for working hard and giving the extra effort. Brooke, I love you and will always be there to support you. You have so much talent, and I look forward to watching you be a mother and build your career. Brooke, I am proud of you! Shanna, Skyla, Jailen, and Sienna – I love you. To brother Doug, thank you for your loyalty; you are the best! I love you Teri, Samantha, Katie Jo and Lauren. To Bill and Megan Fink and Bruce and Laura Pahl, David and Debbie Taylor, Geoff and Debbie Bell, Gary and Lorrie Losse, you guys are great, and I look forward to many more great times. I love you all!!

My involvement with College Basketball has led me to special friendships. The Team of Dente, Spathas, Penrose, Stoney, Goodalls x 2, and Bee has answered the buzzer since 1993 raising almost $2 million to graduate our players. Thanks guys! I will always support coaches Brad Holland, Steve Fisher and Jim Harrick. All three are winners!

"Half-Time." My plan was to publish this book when I turned fifty, optimistically thinking that I would live to be one hundred years old. Today I am 56, but I am eager to see what is in store for me during life's second half. God has a special purpose for my life, as he has for each one of us.

It took me over twenty years to actually share a poem that I had written with another person. Privately I would write what was happening at the time and what was on my mind. It is the collection of those writings that I share in this book "Half-Time." I am hopeful that this book will spark you to write your thoughts down on paper, tell a special person you love them or construct a story. If you do, I hope you will have the courage to share it with another. God bless you.

Very sincerely,
Gregory R. Nelson

# A Note

100% of the proceeds from "Halftime" go to support the Nelson Charitable Foundation and their charities: Fellowship of Christian Athletes, Carlsbad and other Boys and Girls Clubs, University of San Diego Athletic Scholarship Program, San Diego State University Athletic Scholarship Program, La Casa Center for Autism, Casa de Amparo for abused children, Carlsbad High School College Scholarships Grants and other Christian youth-need based organizations.

# Chapter 1

## Happiness, Motivation, Goal Setting

## A Wish for You

I wish for you
Eyes which see good in all
And beauty in the air.

I wish for you
Lips that taste and speak
Of magic everywhere.

I wish for you
Ears that hear of kindness
With not a single sound of despair.

I wish for you much love
And that great feeling to be secure.

But most of all I wish for you
A lifetime of happiness.

*Greg Nelson*

## Positive Attitude

A positive attitude
    Hard to find for some,
They find it easier
    To use a negative one.

Yet once you learn
    To find good in all,
It makes your outlook on life
    Feel so very tall.

And in all you do
    If you feel this way,
You'll wonder why a positive attitude
    Isn't in us all each day.

*Greg Nelson*

## The Challenge

To set your aim upon a star
    Takes more than thinking where you'll be,
And hoping to be there very soon
    Is a wishful, well-sung song and tune.

Reaching high for that brass ring
    Feels good inside – talking of big things,
Wanting more and expecting such
    Verbalizing your plan and wanting it so much.

Now you've thought your way through it
    Down on paper are the steps you'll take,
One challenge is to be the best prepared
    With thoughtful preparation – a goal you will make.

The real challenge is to be different than most
    To go the distance others might not go,
Setting your aim and taking positive steps
    Moving forward with the plan you now know.

Go enthusiastically in your personal direction
    Bring along desire and determination too,
With God's help and support you'll get there
    Because no one can stop you – except you!

*Greg Nelson*

# Just Do It

Hey – let's have more fun!
Let others fret away the day,
Don't worry 'bout what you cannot control
Just move forward and find more time to play.

Why sit in a chair or lie on the couch
Not the boob tube today for me!
I'm gonna make the best of every single day
Our time on earth is precious – rather short and free.

Really, I can't always be serious
I feel sometimes there is little I can do,
I've done enough for now to plan for the future
It's time to put on my running shoes.

If I don't "Get it moving," I know I'll miss out
Enthusiasm is the spark I must keep,
Get psyched up with a positive attitude
Build more excitement and I'll never sink.

If you don't feel like Nike's – "Just Do It!"
And you really would rather just veg,
You still gotta get up and make the effort
'Cause you'll have plenty o' time to lie around
when you're dead.

*Greg Nelson*

## Floor Burns of Life

Life's hustle takes its different turns
When the effort you give is your best,
A new test is always just around the corner
Separating true champions from the rest.

Challenges and obstacles number often and many
Sometimes the odds of winning look bleak,
Reach deep inside you, strengthen your feelings
For throwing in the towel is for the weak.

Floor burns and bruises are part of the ordeal
Can't avoid such when in battle or war,
Believing you have given every amount of effort
Your spirit lies beaten and sore.

It's important to know the truth of your effort
Did you give everything you had?
Did you dive for the loose ball and help your team?
Anything less than 100 percent is sad.

You really can't believe you've given your best
If you don't have some floor burns of life,
Knowing when to reach deep and make a difference
Shows confidence, inner-strength and a feeling of
what is right

*Greg Nelson*

## Success

Some search for it
A whole life through.....

Asking many
Trying to find out whom
Can help them be...
Successful.

What is Success, you may ask.
Can it be put in a class by itself –
or is it an ideal
That we each must make real within?

*Greg Nelson*

## To Our Self Teach

As time flies by and years do too
More often you think deeper – I know,
Days and months pass much faster
Wondering...what to do next...or to go!

Family needs draw more of your attention
Priorities change quickly...seems in a wink,
Clarity unclouds the priority of times that are important
More "quality" time with friends and family you seek.

Life's joys are around you in so many ways
Pleasures that for a time seem good,
Superficial ups lasting only for a moment
Good times with an ending of..."I should".

The most real and true joy is available to all
With need not for money, mortar, or paint,
Family, friends and the Lord's Smiling Eyes
Is the Formula and Road Map to Life's Gate.

So as we move down this life's swift path
Working toward many goals we'll reach!
It's good to stop – if only for a moment
To focus on the real priorities...
to our self teach.

*Greg Nelson*

## The Best Things

Some people work
    Their whole lives through,
Striving forward for money
    With all that they can do.

Working for those material things
    How happy they will be!
But finding out when they get it
    The best things in life are free.

With values reaching
    Up and down the ladder,
And priorities are misdirected
    For some it doesn't matter.

Spending weeks and months
    Sometimes a lifetime too,
Before they finally realize
    The best things in life are free.

*Greg Nelson*

# The Taste of Success

Enjoy your first taste of success
    The feeling of a job well done.
This special sensation filled with excitement
    I couldn't be more proud of you, my son.

You're just now learning about working hard.
    You're now just concentrating on your goals.
Learning to fight through life's many roadblocks
Building confidence – you continue to forward go!

As you compete and try to do well
    Each day a good effort you will make.
Some days it'll be easier – or at least it seems
    And other days you just can't get a break!

On average you'll get back the reward that you earn
    Depends most on your time that is well spent.
Preparing to succeed for the task that you set
    Makes the odds better for success – once again

*Greg Nelson*

# Love

Can come so fast
    And leave the same
But then can it be that it's Love?

With your feelings so strong
    You'll know they'll last long
And then you develop that doubt.

What "IS" love you then ask?
    How much time must then Pass
                Till You Know?

*Greg Nelson*

## Good News!!

Things must not be right
    In the world in which we belong,
For news is only worthy
    When it highlights what is wrong.

You can pick up any newspaper
    Or turn on the nightly news,
What they are always informing us
    Is that the world is in a state of blues.

We are advised of some gruesome murders
    Or read of a war in the East.
Is there no interest in describing the beauty?
    Must our media describe only the beast?

Just once I'd like to pick up the paper,
    Or turn on the nightly news,
And hear only of the world's good side
    This transfusion we all could use!

Wouldn't this be much nicer
    Providing the high points of life's giving,
Drawing a daily example for others to follow
    Promoting the finer points of positive living!

*Greg Nelson*

## Living with Love

Our most natural state
Forgotten early and relearned
is love.

To be happy...joyful...peaceful...each day
    Are feelings when love's shared
With others – giving in your way.

Love is ever plentiful
    It's a well never to be dry
To be spread to all, and eternity
    For God knows love will never die.

Yet love is but a boomerang
    Swirling out so high,
It's impossible to catch it
    Till first thrown freely to the sky

So in our lives from this date
    Giving this gift that's simple but great,
And return to our early and natural state
    And live our lives with love.

*Greg Nelson*

## Happiness Is

Happiness is
    Freedom to Enjoy
        Each day that you live
    To smile at each other
        To share, help and give.

Happiness is
    Falling in love
        With the person of your dreams,
    Who makes you feel happy
        So perfect for you it seems.

Happiness is
    Sharing your life with one,
        Spending quality time together
    Working to make every day fun.

And that special feeling you share
    On your wedding day
        When your life is joined with another.
    This knot is meant to stay
        While your love will grow and grow
    And you'll kiss each night and know
            This Is Happiness!

*Greg Nelson*

# Life's Moguls

Up and down life's endless hills
    Gives balance to us each day,
Like steep moguls on a ski slope
    They make you earn your way.

Life isn't meant to be easy.
    And it isn't here to stay.

But while the moguls of life surround you
    Cheer Up! To yourself you should say –
'Cause at the top of the next big hill
    Is a gentle slope and beautiful day.

*Greg Nelson*

## The Important Stuff

Are we really doing the important stuff?
This question so simple it seems,
But I wonder sometimes if our daily tasks
Get mixed up and in the way of our dreams.

Ask anybody you know – what is more important?
Work, money, family, or friends.
The answer is always – "Family comes first!"
But that is sometimes where this priority ends.

Are we really doing the important stuff?
This individual struggle – an ongoing fight.
We must work hard to provide for our family,
And still keep this priority in sight.

Important Stuff though can take on bigger meanings.
I think the answer to the question really is
Balancing personal needs with work, friends and family
Is the living example to your family you can give.

*Greg Nelson*

## A New Leaf

Let's try to turn over a new leaf
I'm going to be positive all day.
I promise to look at the best side of all
Positive, possibility thinking – I Will Say!

I really don't need a holiday season
Or a special occasion to focus on good,
Every single day can bring you happiness
If we believe deep inside that it could!

The world spins the same all the days of the year
The sun and moon rise, shine, and then rest,
Our attitude, then actions follow forth, too
If we concentrate and work hard to do our best.

Fighting off the negative that will appear
Negativity is a challenge to us all,
It won't be easy to keep on the positive track
With balance and faith you will not fall.

Let's try to turn over a new leaf
Take it just one day at a time,
We already know that any lifelong journey
Starts with a single step so let your new sunrise shine!

*Greg Nelson*

## A Time to Grow

Life is evolutionary
    Time passes as we grow,
For as time passes
    We know not where we go.

A person enters your life
    Like a gift from above,
The key to your heart is stolen
    And you feel love.

You lose your heart again
    Why you do not know,
Never knowing where it went
    Never knowing where it will go.

While life's crystal cloud
    Becomes more dense,
You're still looking for that feeling
    Once sensed.

So you live each day
    One by one,
Searching those special feelings
    That are now undone.

As the evolution of yourself continues
    With your heart locked up so,
You feel it's time to learn
    You know it's time to grow.

*Greg Nelson*

## May Your Every Dream Come True

May the most you wish for
    Be the least you get
May your every dream come true.

Enjoying moments with your family
    Creating friendships that grow,
Filling years with warm memories
    Simple basics we already know.

We work toward our earthly goals
    Sometimes they cloud life's gate,
Might cast a shadow on a value
    Leaving a void in our mental state.

May the most you wish for
    Be the least that you get
May your every dream come true.

We can get ourselves refocused
    We can be all we want to be,
We can set out to make our dreams come true
    From our mind's eye only we can see.

*Greg Nelson*

## Business Partners

When worries come upon us
    Some situations look so bleak,
The time is now to stand up tall
    And turn the other cheek.

While some sit and worry
    And others begin the retreat,
We bow our back and get ready
    For we know we can't be beat.

And cowards die a hundred deaths
    Before their world is done
The brave keep moving forward
    For his only death is one.

*Greg Nelson*

# New Beginnings

New Beginnings bring doubts to each of us
    We're afraid to see what will happen next,
Anxiety builds and emotions overflow
    New beginnings, to me, mean a new test!

It can be a move to a new neighborhood
    Or a strange place to eat or just rest,
A nervous heart beats with every single step
    Eventually you learn new horizons can be the best!

Still major life changes can bring real fears
    A first child, new job or relationship top the list,
We must have faith that change brings opportunity
    And realize some change we just can't resist.

New beginnings can be part of life's treasures
    We learn to adjust to change and such,
But we also should learn to finish what we start
    Can a life of unfinished beginnings be worth very much?

*Greg Nelson*

Personal Notes:

On this page write a few descriptive words or phrases regarding your feelings for effort, attitude, goals or pride.

# Chapter 2
## GOD AND SPIRITUALITY

## Thank You God!

Now and then
    When you're feeling low,
It's hard to think
    Of what others know.

How good you really have it
    All day and each night,
When others may wonder
    If a meal is in sight,
Or if their shelter
    Will last through the night.

Now and then
    It's good for us to think,
About those who are less fortunate
    For those not in the pink.

And count our blessings
    One by one,
For feeling low seems silly
    With all that we have won.

Thank you God!

*Greg Nelson*

## A Personal Inventory

Another day draws to a close
    The lights dim one by one,
Children are lovingly tucked into bed
    Tomorrow brings another day, another sun.

The still of night surrounds you again
    A silence and peace that darkness seeks,
The day is finished forever and ever
    Your deeds for this day have peaked.

Maybe it is a time for reflection
    Maybe it is a time to sleep,
Is it a wishful time of wantings
    Or a peaceful time you're glad to keep?

Darkness before sleep brings a personal time
    We check to see if all the pieces are there
An inventory that only we can know the parts
    For any voids only to ourselves we share.

The puzzle of life includes very few pieces
    But a single piece missing leaves a feeling of not
    whole,
For the God-shaped "peace" of the puzzle
    Can only be filled within from your soul.

*Greg Nelson*

## Counting Blessings

Count your blessings!
    Is easy for us to say,
Couldn't we do this often,
    Shouldn't we do it each day?

All we have to do
    Is open our eyes to see
Those millions of people less fortunate.
    How very lucky are we!

Though holidays bring philosophical thoughts,
    With people smiling and counting blessings all day,
Wouldn't each of us be a little happier,
    If we celebrated Thanks – Giving every day?

*Greg Nelson*

# The Feeling

"The Feeling" to be one with God
A peace that calms one's heart,
It brightens our darkest days
So a whole new world may start.

The light of our Father shines directly to you
His presence surrounds our every move,
This confidence that was never felt before
Is now noticed by others in the same room.

The void in our heart has now been filled
This piece of the puzzle of man,
Can only be complete when God is within
As our Heavenly Father takes me gently by my hand.

"The Feeling" is truly overwhelming
To be cleansed as only He can do,
Please open your heart to let the Holy Spirit come in
He'll bring to you, the feeling of His love, too.

*Greg Nelson*

# Learning to Appreciate

As babies we spend
    Our time expecting,
To get what we need
    With little appreciation.

Then we grow a little older
    And start to realize
How our needs are acquired,
    And we begin to be
Tentatively grateful
    For wants that are fulfilled.

But when we learn to appreciate
    The life God has given us,
We become keenly aware and sensitive
    And experience a clarity of values
Not known to us before
- Because of Appreciation -

*Greg Nelson*

## All Is Seen

Naked are both our body and soul
    Entering into this world as we do,
Only God might know of the life we'll live
    He'll even be there beside us...
        If we want Him to!

We move through our younger years unknowingly
    With the spoken word, actions and thoughts complete,
We're a product of all we think, do and say
    Our own identity and style we will seek.

Mistakes along the way are part of the ordeal
    Hopefully we learn from at least a few,
It is the delicate combination of life's wins and losses
    All added up...
        It's who we are and what we do!

Growing older and better understanding right from wrong
    We are then held more accountable to Thee,
Later errors of judgment and life's trials and tribulations
    Can't be as easily forgiven...
        And ALL IS SEEN!

*Greg Nelson*

## Thanks Again

Moving quickly down a busy road
    Looking at the beautiful sky,
I begin to count my many blessings
    Not quite understanding why.

Why am I the lucky one, I ask
    To rejoice in my life this way,
Having so many of life's things be just so right
    I give thanks...whispering, I pray.

God has given me a healthy family
    He has guided me to a wonderful wife,
Filling most every thought with optimism
    He has a beautiful Blueprint for my Life.

Thanks Again God!

*Greg Nelson*

## Gotta Get It All Together

Gotta get it all together!
To truly find peace in your heart,
You need all the parts overlapping
Can't leave out even one little part.

First a strong spiritual base
A Godly foundation for your tower,
And a healthy body to build on
Stamina, strong will, and personal power!

Need family and friends to share the load
Social time filled with laughter and tears,
Sharing special moments with loved ones
Memories lasting for all your years.

Gotta get it all together!
Means staying mentally alert, too...
With body and soul set firmly
Your brain has more than enough room.

Gotta keep it all together!
Don't let a void last very long,
Keeping a balance in all areas of need
Makes that inner peace feeling strong

*Greg Nelson*

## To Witness

What if you felt you lived a Christian life
Keeping your Godly feelings inside,
Having a private relationship with our God above
But from other people these feelings you hide.

It still works well for you and Him
This peace for yourself you keep,
Not really wondering or caring about others
The love for God in your heart is deep.

But unbelievably it happens – You are arrested
You are charged as being an unbeliever!
Is this a dream or are the charges real?
In this life you were always an achiever.

This "case," the police say will be simple to prove
There is no real evidence of Christian living,
We can't find one single witness to testify
That this person to God his Soul was given.

Wouldn't this be sad if it were true
To live as a Christian all alone,
With not a trace of proof that would clear you
If you were arrested, charged, and brought to
His throne.

*Greg Nelson*

## Building Good Each Day

God gives us all a chance
    To live and our life enhance,
With true happiness the goal for us all.

We spend our time acquiring
    Possessions we later ignore,
Only working again for just a little bit more.

And a handshake is not good enough
    To settle your average deal,
Cause you're never actually sure
    If the person really wants to steal.

Lack of pride is a problem
    Most of us will agree,
Some will avoid work
    If they can get it quickly and free

The truth of the matter is simple
    And some have found the way,
It is easy to reach your goal
    When you build good into every single day.

*Greg Nelson*

## He'll Be Near

The world we live in becomes shaken
When one we love must go.
The why – never to be answered
God shares not to us – only He knows.

It's not for trying to figure out
It's not for a reason of man.
It's best described as the Will of God
Our Lord has taken him by the hand.

This pain felt by family and friends,
Will bring tears of sympathy shared,
It'll sow seeds of closeness and love
In this time of sorrow and despair.

Little problems of daily living seem nothing
When put in perspective of relative thoughts,
Experiencing this sorrow makes us appreciate others.
Must it take a time of sadness to be taught?

Now I move on to a new chapter
As my life continues to unfold.
With some questions I still must move forward
For other loved ones I must be bold!

Past imprints will always remain with me
Memories of this love will bring a tear,
For my family I'll be brave and positive
And pray to God He'll always be near.

*Greg Nelson*

## Thanksgiving Prayer

Thanksgiving started with Pilgrims,
    And their fellowship with the Indians back then,
It was their time to give thanks for their blessings,
    By sharing a feast of a fat-feathered friend.

Now years later here we are
    With family and friends sharing this day,
Counting our blessings each and every one,
    Giving thanks to our Lord Jesus we pray.

We thank you Dear God for our health
    and the friendship and family we share,
We pray that you help strengthen our spiritual lives,
    Because we know for each one of us you care.

Amen

## Christmas

Christmas is celebrated all over the world.
    This day changed us for all time,
Jesus was born in Bethlehem
    Put on earth to save your soul and mine.

Three wise men came to see the newborn,
    Following a bright star in the East,
They brought presents to the King on earth,
    An event Christians will forever teach.

Sent to teach us but not to stay.
    First, he must give his life for us,
God's only Son born on Christmas Day
    Taught the world, "In God You Can Trust."

Now as we enjoy this Christmas holiday season
    Hearing children singing and laughing while at play,
Filled with colored lights, presents and decorated trees,
    Let's try to remember why we celebrate this day.

*Greg Nelson*

Personal Notes:

On this page write a few descriptive words or phrases regarding spirituality and your relationship with God.

# Chapter 3
## FAMILY

## Children Learning

A child learns
    From teachers everywhere,
But learns about a home
    Only when parents are there.

Tasks take longer
    When the little one shares,
But they need to feel
    That these tasks are also theirs.

If this chance is not given
    In the home in which they live,
They probably won't be capable
    When it's their chance to give.

So even when tasks take
    With a child's help much longer,
Your child will learn to work
    And in life will be much stronger.

*Greg Nelson*

## Lucky One

I'm a lucky man
    I heard them say,
The way my lady treats me
    Each and every day.

When she reaches for me
    In the middle of the night,
Then moves a little closer
    Holds me so tight.

She awakens with a smile
    Goes to bed that evening the same,
There's little doubt that I'm a winner
    In life's mating game.

I love her so
    She's the only one for me,
But I'm not the only one that's lucky
    'Cause so is she.

*Greg Nelson*

## To My Children

To each of my children
    I hope and pray,
That your life is filled with happiness
    Each minute, hour and day.

To my individual children
    So proud of who they are,
Secure in what they stand for
    Their integrity without a mar.

To my compassionate children
    Caring for others in need,
Helping and holding out a hand to touch
    For those less fortunate whom your heart bleeds.

To my learned children
    Searching for knowledge your way,
May not a single day pass before you
    Without learning something new to think, or say.

To my proud children
    If you always do your best,
And complete those things you said you'd do
    Your reputation will take care of the rest.

To my loving children
    Who are an extension of me,
May you find the truth as I did
    What really matters in life is free.

*Greg Nelson*

## Our Loan

My children are growing up too fast
 Years seem to fly on by,
Their days of youthful innocence numbering fewer
 With these thoughts, a tear builds in my eye.

I learned years ago about the loan of youth
 A loan God grants to parents like me,
Children are born and allowed to grow up with us
 Until they are ready to be set free.

Picturing the moments...those special ones
 With a smile in our mind's eye we remember,
Is a gift from God that only parents can know
 When we were a family all living together.

*Greg Nelson*

## Sounds of Children

Enjoying the sounds of children's activities
In boys and girls as they grow,
Is a major part and special gift,
For moms and dads in the know.

To hope for peace and quiet
Is only for those not so real,
Having the time with your children,
Surely is one of life's big deals!

This time will pass by quickly,
When for children, your time they'll seek,
As the adult years grow nearer and nearer,
The shade of time with them dims bleak.

Best to smile and enjoy every moment!
Even as innocent at the time it seems,
'Cause it's a big part of a quality life,
And fond memories and a happy heart
Will fill your dreams.

*Greg Nelson*

## In My Arms Again

As the sun comes up in the morning
    And you're still in my arms,
What a beautiful start for a day.

Our love has grown yet another step
    To be remembered as we go on our way.

And as the day progresses
    While each of us addresses
Our own and separate kind of world,
    I look forward with delight
'Cause I know that very night
    You'll be in my arms again.

*Greg Nelson*

## Tough Love

Nobody said that it would be easy.
Nobody said you would always be kind,
Nobody said that being a parent
Would mean difficult decisions and much restless time.

I think they call it parental "tough love"
When it's time to cut the cord,
When it's time to stand alone
Putting them now in the hands of the Lord.

It's a time for their independence.
It's a time to be set free,
Now their life on this earth as a person
Will only be an extension of me.

You hope a good foundation has been built.
You hope they know a wrong move from one right,
You hope that most of life's lessons to date
Are now available to help smooth this new flight.

Of course, you will be there to help
And give love and a little support if they should need,
But the tough love part of our place as a parent
Is not for us – but so that our children will be free!

*Greg Nelson*

## Valentine's Day

Loving you sweetheart is easy
    Feelings for you continue to grow,
I still get excited – just to see you
    How deep is my love? You know!

You bring much joy to many
    Always willing to give smiles and helping hands,
With an open heart and an abundance of energy
    You're a good person to help your fellow man.

By example you teach the art of giving
    Caring for those who need,
You're an angel certainly sent from heaven
    Contributing to many at God's speed.

You have arrived here for this purpose
    One that is surely designed from Above,
How very proud I am just to share life with you
    For me you are my special earthly love.

I don't really need a Valentine's Day
    To tell me what to do,
Designated days might be important for some
    But for me each day is Valentine's Day with you!

*Greg Nelson*

June 18, 1992

Chad,

It is hard to believe the time is here,
    You're graduating from Carlsbad High!
Seems only yesterday when I took my little boy
    To first grade, with a tear in my eye.

So many wonderful experiences we've shared since,
    Twelve grades have passed by with a flash,
Being with you, while you've grown, has been such a joy,
    Did it have to go by so darn fast?

Remembering Pop Warner bowls and little league games,
    All star tourneys and basketball most everywhere,
Always watching that quick, little blond boy.
    I hope you knew, if I could, I was there!

You have accomplished much in your first 18 years,
    Both athletic and leadership awards put you on top,
Chosen the county's #1 player and athlete of the year
    Everybody knew you were the cream of the crop!

You've grown into such an outstanding young man,
    No father in the world is prouder than me.
Combining sensitivity, competitiveness, goodness, and poise
    Your popularity draws a crowd just to see.

It's time now to move forward on your journey,
To new challenges set before you in this life.
With a positive attitude and hard work you'll make it.
Stay persistent with your goal always in sight!

With much love and support,
Dad

April 11, 1996

To Brooke

Seems only yesterday
    When this now big girl was born,
She's turning 18 and graduating high school
    My heart is both happy and torn.

For her I am excited
    'Cause she's already chosen the next turn in life's road,
She'll be attending a college in San Luis Obispo
    Leaving her nest – Now her own seeds she'll sow.

It is hard to accept that she is an adult
    This baby girl I helped name Brooke,
For the times we had together passed by so quickly
    And a big piece of my heart she took.

Can't spend much time focusing on the "I Wishes"
    Because the only thing that matters for her now,
Is the knowledge that her daddy truly loves her
    And will always be there to help – if she'll allow.

Brooke, I wish for you a life filled with health and happiness
    I wish for you your own family full of love,
And I pray you will find a spiritual togetherness

With your Heavenly Father who loves you from above.

So now move on forward to your new world
Remember, you can reach any goal you set,
By gathering together your strong will and ability
You'll be successful, I'm willing to bet!

With much love,
Dad

## Graduation Day 2002 - Gregory

Looking back at the many memories
Special times and moments through the years,
Brings to my heart a wonderful, warm feeling
But brings to my eyes loving, happy tears.

With such pride I share with you this day
Graduating now from Carlsbad High,
It is time to let you free to soar
It is time to let you fly!

Remembering the joy we felt when you were born
Proud parents were both mom and I
We loved you, nurtured you, as Chad did, too
I think he cared for you as much as we.

You grew up to be every person's friend
Respected and liked by all that came in touch,
I could not be more proud of who you are
Gregory – I love you so very much.

Your efforts and style have brought you success
A showstopper and basketball star you are,
But your love of God, compassion, and integrity
Will be life's habits that take you far.

Most Valuable Player of the Basketball League and Torrey Pines, too
    The first ever CHS four-year basketball starting guard,
Are part of the recognition thus far you have earned
    Because you did what was right and worked very hard.

Now as you move forward to the challenges ahead
    I am confident you will give it your best,
College life will surely give you a few bumps and bruises
    But Gregory, I know you are up to the test.

With much Love,
Dad

## Sweet Sixteen

January 20th, 2002

God has given me many gifts on this earth
But none more precious than you,
At any age you will always be my "princess"
And I will always try to be that "king" to you.

Today you will turn a sweet sixteen
I'm sure "sweet sixteen" and never been kissed
It's been wonderful for Mom and me to watch you grow
But our "baby girl" Jenna will surely be missed.

I am so proud of the person you have become
The confident, wonderful young lady that you are
With a smile on my face I watch you mature
But I remember "Butterfly Kisses," – a time now not so afar.

Sixteen, as you know, is a big birthday for you
Promises that you will finally get to go on a date!
But you are well aware of the difficult rules in our home
Even now, you can't stay out too late!

I look forward to sharing the many years ahead
Finishing high school, then college and the such,
I know whatever you do, you will always keep a level head
And will always know your mother and father love you so very much.

Happy 16th Birthday!

Love Dad

## Watching Him Grow

His face is starting to chisel
    Into a nice-looking young man.
I've watched him grow from the beginning.
    He's made me his number one fan.

Already thirteen in his life's long race.
    Hard to believe that it's already so.
Yet he's not too big to cuddle on the couch
    When his active social schedule slows.

Gregory, my boy!  He shares my name.
    I love our very special tie.
He can brighten up even the dullest of times
    With his friendly smile and those great big eyes.

It's a unique combination of characters
    That make up this talented and versatile lad.
As a fierce competitor, he can really get mad,
    To the boy in the bubble bath who says "It isn't all bad."

I look forward to sharing the many years ahead
    With my boy as I watch him grow.
Knowing that God has a plan for him
    We'll wait and see where God wants him to go.

*Greg Nelson*

## My Princess

She will always be my princess.
    I will always be her king,
It sounds so very corny
    When we say to each other "our thing."

As I tuck her in each night with a kiss
    Wishing her a good night's sleep,
Reminding her to say her prayers,
    And ask God for her soul to keep.

Jokingly, "What color Porsche do you want,
    When you turn your sweet 16?"
Answering, "Any color you like Daddy,"
    In my ears her teasing clearly rings.

I'm sure I won't always be her "king"
    As she grows into a woman, I suppose,
But I'll always think of her as my princess
    Watching her charge forward to her life's goals.

*Greg Nelson*

## Growing Up!

Dad: At times things seem so unfair
Everything seems stacked against you,
The harder you try, thinking you're falling short,
Wondering if somebody's cheating you!

Son: I didn't do anything really bad!
I think my friends were acting worse!
Why does everybody always blame me?
Am I stuck with some kind of curse?

Dad: Learning to win at life's lessons,
It might be the hardest thing to do,
'Cause everybody makes mistakes,
And I really don't like to see you blue.
Everyone in the world has their bad days,
Some a little more than the next.

Son: I am really trying to be good,
Most times I'm trying my very best!

Dad: Son, even when times seem so tough,
And some things aren't coming together,
You've got to reach deep within you,
And know that for you things will get better.
And they do!

*Greg Nelson*

## A Note from Dad

Even though single events in life may not seem fair at the time, your life in the long run will be a result of the effort you put forth each day.

Living for the day is a mistake. But enjoying each day while planning for the future brings you both joy and a sense of security.

Giving 100 percent effort in everything you do is impossible in human behavior. But raising your personal level of pride to your "highest level" is important for your satisfaction. Then all you attempt is measured against your level of pride. This will help you answer the question, "Who Am I?"

Most every day you live, participate in an activity that further develops your Mind/Academia, Spiritual Awareness and Body. For without all three, life will be less Fruitful.

Always remember that I Love You very much and am proud of each of you!

*Greg Nelson*

Personal Notes:

On this page write a few descriptive words or phrases regarding your feelings for your family, children or friends.

Personal Notes:

On this page write a few descriptive words or phrases regarding your feelings for your spouse or another.

# Chapter 4
# Sports

## Teamwork

Teamwork can be traced to most every success story
'Cause few deeds are accomplished alone,
Any tough challenge will be most often achieved
When teamwork – The Spirit of a Team – is shown.

The momentum of any single-minded force
Is hard for anything or anybody to stop,
Such energy garnered by people working together
Will put most teams over the top!

Every player must know well his position
Every player should know the plan,
Every player must be ready to help others
Part of teamwork is helping your fellow man.

First you have to decide for yourself
Because teamwork means "Doing Your Part,"
Doing what's good and remembering
There is no "I" in team
Is a great start!

*Greg Nelson*

## Winning Moment

A Dream is but a dream
    Until it comes true for you.
Hoping and praying for the chance
    Doing everything you can do.

Others may see it as a fantasy.
    Some do not believe that you can,
You're still unwilling to change direction,
    Confidently going forward – this young man.

With hustle and heart, you plow on through
    Winning one small battle after one,
Sustaining the will that few can match.
    Thankfully, this war is won!

Enjoy now this winning moment.
    Feel good about what you have done,
No one can take it back from you.
    You set the target – ran forward – and won!

*Greg Nelson*

## Stars Aren't Always Bright

In any other line of work
    If a man choked his boss,
He'd be looking for another job.
    Immediate termination would be the verdict – for
    cause.

But not for our high-priced athletes
    Laws and society's rules are not for them,
Since most live with their own code of conduct,
    If there's trouble they have an agent, attorney and
    union to send.

Whether they wish to or not they can't help it!
    Young people everywhere follow their "moves",
Might be their dribble or how they run the football
    Or an endorsement for a new style of shoes.

It's really too bad how pro sports have turned out.
    An embellished example of what society has become,
When a combination of money spent and a strong denial
    Can change wrong to "right" in public battles for some.

For parents and teachers each and everywhere
    It's a little harder to teach our boys and girls,
When time and time again examples of fairness and trust
    Get ignored, under disciplined or over-ruled!

*Greg Nelson*

## Saturday Mornings

A few guys are thrown
    Together this day,
To work up a sweat
    Jumping, shooting, and running they play.

In this cold empty gym
    They come from near and far
Each hoping to play good enough to win
    Before they get back into their car.

Playing like the "Good 'Ole Days"
    Some still showing class,
While always there are few
    Who run out of gas.

For most of the guys it's exciting
    When you walk on through this door,
'Cause each knows how sad it'll be
    When we can't play anymore.

*Greg Nelson*

## The Road to Final Four

March Madness brings us many moments
Excitement that covers our entire land,
Basketball fever taken to the limit
Building anxiety into every fan.

Cheering for your favorite teams,
Alumni bragging after their win,
63 teams must be eliminated.
A few close to what might have been.

Final Four is the thrill of it all.
The hoopla that surrounds every team's moves,
All eyes looking forward to Monday's championship game.
It's sad – but one more team has to lose.

Every year I bet on the tournament games
This year I lost miserably bad to Jack,
I think that he got a little bit lucky
So next year for March Madness, I'll be back!

*Greg Nelson*

# Chapter 5

## Seasons, Comments on Our World

## Caribe Vacation

There's nothing quite like a Caribbean Vacation
To get you rested and back in touch,
What a great place to get away from it all
You'll enjoy the peacefulness very much.

Seems the sun is always shining
The white sand so fine – but hot,
With lush tropical gardens, a paradise
There can't be on earth more beautiful spots.

The locals are friendly and all "hang loose,"
"No Problem Mon" the answer you so often hear,
Kick back, rest and enjoy the simple time
"Red Stripe Please," just one more beer.

Island Music so freely filled with rhythm
A Beat to me a bit like rap,
But don't get excited about island-to-island shopping
It might be a different island...
But it's the same ol' crap.

*Greg Nelson*

## Springtime

Springtime brings with it much happiness
    In many different ways,
Flowers everywhere start coloring
    And we start living longer days.

The moon seems to shine more brightly.
    Bird choirs sing a chorus of fun,
People everywhere start getting into action
    It's time to plan – how will we enjoy the sun?

For the youngsters, the countdown begins.
How many days of school to go?
And the older folks living in the North
    Are glad to get behind another year of snow.

Spring weddings and celebrating anniversaries
    Are a loving part of this time of year,
And the culmination of years of hard work and persistence
    Gives the graduate a reason to cheer.

Springtime to me means happiness
    For all the reasons listed above,
But also because it means more family activities,
    Time with friends and the family I love.

*Greg Nelson*

# Fall

It is great to feel Fall in the air
When the first cool wind hits your face,
Checking out your wood supply
Hoping you'll get to use the fireplace.

How glad are we when the warm weather is gone
No more fans and air conditioners to hear,
Won't miss that sticky humidity either.
Oh my gosh! The Holiday Season is near!

Leaves are falling and blowing from lawns to streets.
It grows darker a little faster every day,
Children are hurrying home from school
To get in their few lighted hours of play.

Seems that families gather together a bit more
At activities, the dinner table, and TV too,
But the telephone now is dominated by the teens
Weekends are filled with football for a few.

It seems that Fall comes and goes more quickly
Than any of the other seasons I know,
It just seems like this beautiful time of our year
Is a small slice between Summer and the opening of
Winter's door.

*Greg Nelson*

## Remembering "Olde Carlsbad"

The sun has set below the ocean view
    Stars peek out one by one,
The lights of Carlsbad begin to twinkle
    In this small town, another day is done.

Remembering back to the days of Elm Street
    Not a traffic signal could you see,
We would stop by for a 5¢ Wonder Bread store cupcake
    Today, that building is the Carlsbad Brewery.

You climbed down then, to one of a hundred paths to the beach
    A dirt ramp at State Beach and Tamarack stairs worked too,
The Union Church and Old St. Pat's were for Sundays
    It was the only time I wasn't wearing my Converse tennis shoes.

The library then was a small building on Harding
    Novack's Burgers was the best place by the beach to eat,
And I remember Tastee Freeze across from the Royal Palms Chapel
    Was the lunch hangout that couldn't be beat!

Then I was too young to get into Peanuts Bar
    Heard that Ralph and Eddie's was the place for cards,
And the Carlsbad Journal building seemed so big on the corner.

This was way before the infamous "Bars."

The Boys Club was the place just for boys
I don't remember much about what the girls had to do,
The Girls Club since has grown large on Eureka
Carlsbad School busses took us annually to Disneyland
and to the zoo.

There wasn't a "village" anywhere in the neighborhood
But the Royal Palms and the Twin Inns were there,
Great fried chicken and really terrific corn fritters
Was not just a Sunday treat or special fare.

You could get most anything then at McDonald's
Pharmacy
First-run movies like the Alamo played at the State
Street Theater,
And Marja Acres was home to the real chickens
It's the Country Store now and feeds us even better.

The park behind the Twin Inns seemed always empty
I never understood when I was young what it was for,
Until one day, I was helping plan my own wedding
And in the white gazebo I sang to my bride "MORE,"

Over the years there have been many changes
I'm glad I can remember how it used to be,
Today, this city of Carlsbad still remains special
It's no wonder that people come from far and wide
just to see.

I laugh when I hear complaints of congestion
    I smile when I hear of the increase in crowds,
'Cause most of us had to move here from someplace else
    And it is not fair to say now, that I'm here, keep every-
body else out!

*Greg Nelson*

## DonJoy (Now DJ Ortho, NYSE)

From the time when you were born
    To the moment I set you free,
You were always a joy to work with
    For so many others, but mostly me.

Together we had some ups and downs
    At times I doubted you would last,
But looking back over all the years
    The time with you passed so fast.

The garage and the first few buildings
    Seemed to fill up no matter how big,
Sometimes the orders seemed to pour in
    Other times we just had to really dig.

I'll miss the team most of all
It took each member to win the game,
No matter what in the world happens next
    I doubt it can ever be the same.

From babe all the way to adolescence
    Raising you has been a joy,
Imagine the kind of great athlete you'd be
    If, instead of a business, you were a boy!

Now it's time to stand all alone
    You're a strong team – I hope you grow,
After seventeen years you should be ready
    I've taught you all I know!

*Greg Nelson*

# The Good 'Ol Days

Just look around and see
How much the world has changed.
We open our eyes a little wider now
Moving hastily on our way.

Most adults would rather have a more simple style
To live the life that we live,
But we weave our web of countless activities.
Time and money are what mostly we give.

People are choosing to talk less to each other.
They would rather stare at a computer screen,
Some are wearing a device on their self
To be better in touch when they cannot be seen.

And driving down the road in your car
Used to be relaxing and filled with tunes,
Now we have to have our "hands free" cell phones
To tell the next commitment, "I'll be there soon."

We write our notes and letters to others
Sent not by mail but instead by e-mail or fax.
Even the U.S. government got in the act.
We can now use a computer to file our tax!

But years from now we'll look on back
To the "slower times" that went by so fast,
We'll remember "Those Good 'Ol Days."
When times were more simple...in the past.

*Greg Nelson*

## The Beach House

A peacefulness transcends this home
On each board, rock, and brick,
The ocean's movement and birds that soar
This feeling for a lifetime will stick.

Surfers "cutting through" to the ocean's waves,
Walkers looking up to the stairs, path and sky,
This true paradise to all who know
Will be appreciated more as time goes by.

On the vine the grapes would hang
In the atrium a purity you could sense,
Many levels of resting for family, friends and guests
Bringing forward thoughts – what in this life is best?

A beautiful beach home shared by a few
Filled with quality life from corner to corner,
Now makes a picture only in our mind's eye
As we recall the memories and grow older.

*Greg Nelson*

## Mother Teresa and Di

Seventy years of serving the poor
Living with stability and faith while working her plan,
Mother Teresa, a saint on this earth,
Working tirelessly for her fellow man.

Princess Diana, a celebrity who drew attention to her cause
Tried hard to make changes for some,
While at the same time raising her two sons
Preparing for when their time to reign will come.

In the same week we lost them both.
An accident that shocked the world took Di
And just days later God took Calcutta's mother.
Only He knows why they both now had to die.

The media then fed on the royal feast.
People everywhere laid down flowers and cried,
But most of the hype was spent on the Princess
Reliving her sixteen years of celebrity until she died.

Mother Teresa spent a lifetime of self-sacrifice
But was put to rest with less pomp and circumstance,
Undoubtedly, she'll be missed by millions of people.
Her years of serving the poor stretched seven decades and not by chance.

*Greg Nelson*

# Kodiak

Onward to Kodiak to fish with my Son
An adventure and special memory this would be
Halibut and salmon fishing deep in the wilderness
What kind of wildlife would we see?

Larry arranged this trip to be with his sons
Inviting others to come along and enjoy,
Traveling on float-planes to fly fish together
Sounds like the perfect experience for me, my son and the boys.

So we packed our fishing gear and the layers of clothes
Excited for the adventure, not knowing what to expect,
Then when we saw the cabin and lodge where we'd stay
We smiled...shrugged...said "What the heck!"

No need to change clothes and optional showers too
Fishing, playing games, and driving ATV's all day,
Friendships grew on the ocean, streams and lodge
This was time for both big boys and small boys to play.

In Saltry Cove, with Grif, Jenny, their gang and ours
Wild horses, bald eagles, bears and foxes are memories we all share,
Looking back to the beautiful island of Kodiak, Alaska
We'll be happy when we smile and say, "I was there!"

*Greg Nelson*

## Half Time

What a Special and Wonderful Surprise
To Celebrate this, my 50th Year,
Can't imagine anything better to share
With the Friends I hold so dear.

Onward to Napa Valley we went
Both Day and Evening filled with Fun,
Visiting Vineyards and again meeting the Mondavi's
Tasting Great Wines under the Sun.

Experiencing a Once in a Lifetime Cave Dinner
Echoing with Laughter and Heartfelt Tears,
I feel like the luckiest Man on Earth
At least for this first fifty years!

With God looking over me all along the way
Never ever letting me out of his sight,
Teaching me more about Patience and being Thankful
And particularly about enjoying the precious parts of Life

Hopefully Family and Friends will always be a Focus
With Barbi helping to lead me – Hand in Hand
As I hit this mark which I call "Half Time"
I wonder what's next – In God's Plan.

*Greg Nelson*